IN SEARCH OF HOME

CHRIS CONSIDINE

INDEPENDENT INNOVATIVE INTERNATIONAL

Published by Cinnamon Press
Meirion House,
Glan yr afon,
Tanygrisiau,
Blaenau Ffestiniog,
Gwynedd, LL41 3SU
www.cinnamonpress.com

The right of Chris Considine to be identified as author of this work has been asserted by her in accordance with the Copyright, Designs and Patent Act, 1988. Copyright © 2015 Chris Considine.
ISBN: 978-1-909077-53-9

British Library Cataloguing in Publication Data. A CIP record for this book can be obtained from the British Library.

Designed and typeset in Palatino by Cinnamon Press
Cover from original artwork 'Plymouth with a Rainbow' by Joseph Mallard William Turner © Fundacao Calouste Gulbenkian. Used with kind permission.
Cover design by Jan Fortune

Printed in Poland

Cinnamon Press is represented in the UK by Inpress Ltd www.inpressbooks.co.uk and in Wales by the Welsh Books Council www.cllc.org.uk

Acknowledgements

'A Feasting Presence full of Light', 'Strange Strand', 'The Meet' and 'Yachts in Fog' were published in *Envoi*, 'Bay-Window Triptych' appeared in *Artemis* and 'The Voyage Back' in *The Interpreter's House*.
'Pig-sitting on the Island' won 2nd prize in the Cornwall Contemporary Poetry Competition.
'Departure' was chosen as one of the "Poems on the Buses" in the Guernsey Poetry Competition and 'The Uncertainty Principle is Inherent in the Properties of all Wave-like Systems' was a prizewinner in the Torbay Open Poetry Competition.

Biography

Chris Considine is a poet and former school-teacher who lived for many years in Swaledale, North Yorkshire, before moving to Plymouth in 2011. Her publications include *St. Cuthbert and Bystanders* (Redbeck Press, 2001) and *Swaledale Sketchbook* (Smith/ Doorstop Books, 2002) which was shortlisted for the Forward Prize in the best first collection category in 2002. Her first full collection, *Learning to Look*, was published by Peterloo Poets in 2003, followed by *Quarll*, also from Peterloo, in 2006. *Behind the Lines* was published by Cinnamon Press in 2011.
At the beginning of 2004 she was a Hawthornden Fellow.

Contents

To
Jane, Mike, Paul, Carole, Elizabeth, Jean and Bill,
friends and fellow poets

In Search of Home

Home I

1. Revisiting

She raps on the transparent panel of the door.
The knock is soundless. She is invisible
this morning, the black stealth car
not hers, not known here and the road empty.

Unseen unless the hills have eyes
and remember her from her daily wanderings –
her, me, but I look out across the ocean
at the other end of England.

She in her carapace of the past peers in
at the window through dazzled glass.
Hers and not hers – the floor uncarpeted,
half-finished alterations in the kitchen,

the wrong curtains, ugly, not what she chose
and left here. Always a house of shadows; today
the tricky sunlight hardly penetrates,
the rooms are sleeping, under an enchantment.

She could be in one of those dreams where you cry out
but no noise comes. Her house and not hers, same and changed,
mine and not mine, though so long lived with
in light and dark, cloud or clear air, us against the world.

2. The Homecoming

An unlit winding road, hazy moon suggesting
hills. The driver doesn't know where he is destined
but I know. The road narrows, steepens.

No lights in the house, no sound when we stop
and I get out, but I know
this is home. The driver is reluctant

to leave me there but I push through the thorns
of silence grown high since my long ago
departure. Will the door swollen with damp

open to my key? What will I find on the icy flagstones:
dust, feathers, a hundred years of mail?
Shall I come upon myself in a curtained room

sleeping off some spell or illness? Cold ashes in the grate,
sunk into themselves. I stand on the threshold wondering
if I'm returning from an afterlife.

3. Blissful Captivity

Rasselas's happy valley – I imagine it
like the inside of that extinct volcano's crater,
gone green with vegetation climbing up
the nearly vertical sides and waterfalls
bounding down to make the whole enclosure lush.

Here too the green hills wall us in.
The long road out, slow and winding, blocked
sometimes by flood, snow or subsidence
protects us from the east. The bony land,
beautiful but intractable, preserves our quiet.

Easy to understand what danger, rage and misery
we're escaping from here with our backs to the high ground.
But Rasselas was not content either inside
his safe haven or out. Shepherds he found glum
and insular, and the hermit's peace felt like emptiness.

4. Air Island

Island of air in the upper dale,
round-bellied body of air almost enclosed
in the oval of surrounding slopes,

island out of our element – we can only
peer in wistfully as if through a window
at a dimension we are not equipped for.

Like one of those glassy domes that can be shaken
and sometimes it's thistledown or yellow leaves
that fly, but mostly birds:

a bunch of lapwings flapping and tumbling,
or the rapid arcs of swallows,
or curlews and their voices arrowing across,

other times, like a child's Christmas toy,
what's shaken is snow, feathery flakes
meandering down or up, hardly heavier than air,

or rain billowing or gauze of mist – but then
the curved air is a fortune-teller's crystal.
Don't touch – wait for the ghost-shapes to declare themselves.

5. Unclear

That day at sea in a small boat
a ring of clarity around us
then nothing, a colourless blank.

The tiny world of us.
Is there life out there? How
could we make contact?

Driving over the hill last night
in the dark in the fog I recognised
nothing. Which was road, which was not-road

ditch or drop? No white line
cat's-eye, reflector, no streetlamp
no vehicle no lit window –

this place familiar as the back of my hand.
Today there are shifts and changes. Now the smudge
of a tree. Now a hilltop

with a smoky garland.
Fog says trust nothing.
You are alone.

6. An Ark

Hilltop, the highest house, stone ark.
mice in the wall
rats in the logstore
cats in the kitchen
Insidious is a word that sounds like rain,
rain that goes on and on, incessant rain.
Insidiously, surreptitiously,
the river eases out of its constriction.
two flies
two woodlice
two butterflies asleep in the curtains
I wake up to a yellow world. The rain
has paused for breath, but where there should be grass
there's a gold-plated lake, a lid over the lost
villages. The farmer won't come up today.
two cattle from the shed
two sheep by the gate
two chickens from the yard
two dogs from the keeper's barn
It's dark at noon. Like mountains upside-down
clouds dangle heavy peaks.
Trees are out of their depth. New springs surprisingly
spurt from the shrinking slope.
owls crows pheasants grouse
ducks that have risen with the river
slow-worms and frogs
stoats and rabbits
moles and hedgehogs
Electricity's off but we won't be short of water.
With my menagerie I'll sit it out
as long as possible
listening to the hissing on the roof.

7. Mother's Last Christmas

Not the last of her life but the last
when she could cope with freedom,
an unfamiliar room.

We drove over the moor in a blizzard,
held our breath on the dips and rises,
the old house a longed-for refuge.

No neighbours, no lights from distant farms,
no birdcalls, even the snow fell
in a windless silence

and froze silently. There was
no going out on Christmas Day
to the plain brown chapel

where if there were no kings
there would be shepherds,
and three girls playing brass instruments –

mother and I confined to our stone shelter,
our fire, tête-à-tête meals
and radio. No visits

no visitors. Every morning I trudged
the half-mile to the sharp steep curve
gleaming with untouched ice

and every evening at the open door
described to my blind listener
the silver moon, the unreachable silver hills.

8. No Man is an Island

though at the same time we all are,
not even sure if anyone
else exists except as figment
of our fear or longing. Today

it's clear I'm alone, the only
island in white so absolute
it's almost dark. Could it be that
a blind person sees white, not black?

Field walls are drowned in drifts.
If I open my front door
it keeps its icy frieze. I stay
in so as not to break the snow.

My unmarked bubble of whiteness
is a skull I live inside, like a found
sheep's skull scoured to its essence,
in a deep silence

heightened by small rustlings of breath
and blood. Blind, deaf, how could someone
be reached? Rare for another
hand or lip to approach and touch.

Flying Westward

(the day/night map)

The world's rectangular
headed and underlined
by ice-stripes – corridors
to the flat earth's end.

The small familiar continents
and islands, eggshell blue,
float in a turquoise sea,
my country at the centre

a little bitten remnant.
All land scoured by some latter flood
clean of human defacement:
cities gone, and every destination.

And from the east the shadow grows.
Our flying dust's buoyed on night's breath that goes
forward ahead of it
for ever through the empty light.

In the Butterfly Garden at Changi Airport

Disguised in drab, hanging like heavy buds
or seed-pods, then one day yellowing
as if touched by light.

There has been a breaking-down of self
and desire, resurrection of the body into something
quite different

a rebirth that will not be remembered.
That splitting-apart feeling known to women
in labour.

Air on new skin. The ruched wings drop
out of their crinkles, the enfolding garment
coming to life.

Sap stiffens the conduits in the thin membrane
with a slight vibrato – it is like a hand
tentatively

reaching out, finger-ends all sensation.
Is this a long hour for the butterfly, disorientation,
tingling discomfort

or in a kind of wonder a gradual acceptance of grace?
The wings are spread across the air now. Imagine
the letting go.

The Voyage Back

Did I see them or only want to?
Looking towards the sun was difficult
over an indigo sea with running sparkles.
The ship's engines quietened

passengers moved to the starboard side
and someone pointed. I think there was
broken water among the confusion of lights,
perhaps a sliding smoothness

as dark and shining as the sea
inside the oblong of disturbance,
as of something suspended at the surface.
Did I imagine an exhalation of spray?

Word went round: two of them,
humpback mother and calf, swimming so tight
together they might have been touching.
But was this experience or hearsay?

It must have been like that with miracles.
The short-sighted, the ones further back
saying *What can you see?* like
the blind man in the art gallery.

Sea Change

(Shipwrecked in the Torres Strait in 1844, Barbara Thompson lived for five years among the Kaurareg)

I found her sea-sucked white as bone, whiter
than the sand she lay on in her outstretched hair.
I could see she had been dead. I don't think
she will stay – I think they will want her back.
They had wound her in sea-colour. When I
tipped her, brine spouted from her like a spring

washing all words out. Her eyes were estranged
silver as ocean when the sun has gone.
Her whiteness was not salt, though she tasted
salty. Undersea spirits had stolen
her colour and her love. She was empty

except of fear. My lost daughter long since
lost at sea had forgotten her own name.
The women have undone her watery
cloths. She imitates them as if she were
a creature from another element

and like that she fears the sun. It turns her skin
to blood-colour and burns like fire. But still
the brine seeps out of her in tears. Slowly
she learns to live again – to dig and fish
and forage. Slowly her body darkens
but her eyes still look like sea, seawards.

Inselberg

An upturned basin of rock, bare
smooth and still warm though the sun

has gone and the endless green
cumulus the mound looked down on

has made itself invisible.
There are no biting flies this high

so they have brought their sleeping bags outside –
stone has no hardness for them lying

lip to lip almost and quoting poetry
two millennia old, the dead words

coming alive in their mouths, but they're not afraid
of the poet's *nox perpetua* – night seems

bright enough and their island rock
balanced on wilderness immune to time.

Cicadas' sleepy chant runs through them
and around them like a pulse-beat.

Strange Strand

I remember
we went over water like a mirror
under a blinding sky in an open boat.
Hot, windless and strangely silent.
And then the trek through the shadows of the forest.
What we had arrived at was not quite an island:
it seemed to be a place off the edge of the world.
The green glass ridges of the sea came in, came in
and a million splinters glittered on the shore –
the sand was bright as fire
our feet burned, our eyes were dazzled,
salt air too sharp to breathe.
Love, this was not a place where life could be sustained –
air sharp with salt, feet burning, eyes dazzled, sand bright as fire
and a million splinters glittering on the shore
as green glass ridges of the sea came in, came in.
It seemed to be a place off the edge of the world,
what we had arrived at – not quite an island.
And then the trek through the shadows of the forest
hot, windless and strangely silent.
Under a blinding sky in an open boat
we went over water like a mirror.

I remember.

Home II

1. Downsizing

The dining-room is untidy
with boxes of her husband's books.
In the kitchen, one is propped on its spine
to set the glue in its delicate leather.

Upstairs a wastepaper basket
overflows with Greece, Crete, Istanbul
1962, in tiny transparencies
and school magazines full of remembered names.

She feels guilty about her mother's
thin Victorian cups, the blanks
in the china cabinet. Yesterday Oxfam.
Tomorrow the auction rooms in Leyburn

where she will not get much.
Things weighed her down
but as she dismantles her past
their loss seems even heavier.

2. Home

By the waters of Babylon there I sat down,
yea I wept when I remembered Swaledale.
Watching the busy shipping in the Sound:
the little boats like insects to and fro,
the high white ferry, the returning frigate,
home, but to go again, to go again.

How many houses have I lived in?
Always looking out, to trees,
street, hills, sea, other houses on and on,
but looking from. The world framed and limited
through the eyes of the house.

As if the soft body needed the house's armour.
As if the body accommodated itself
to the house's corners and exigencies,
longing to share its roots.

When I've lost a house I dream of it:
of that room with its white walls, its wooden ceiling
like the lid of a box; of my bedroom
with the scuffling of mice in the walls,
the banging wind, owl voices under the moon.
I have dreamt of the empty garden at Westover,
of Gunfield and Venn, the wet getting in,
plaster softening, paper peeling
in strips like skin; my nights spent
in fear for these abandoned houses.

Here on earth have we no continuing home
but we seek one to come, seek one to come.
A poor translation, and without Brahms' music
for that second line, the sense only half there;
what grips the heart: simple longing
on the first *seek* but the repetition
minor, more tentative – we grow out of
comfort blankets. Home, after all, an earthly word.
From this to that we move, still seeking.

I envy the farmers of the dale, ancestrally
linked to the land, the house's stones.
To look out at the same hill (infinitely variable)
child, youth, man; for it to be both first and last,
looking back at you, at your own variations.

Beside the bland water, grey now under cloud,
I grieve for my house on the white hill
its roof and yard weighted with cold, its narrow road
lost under days of fallen crystals,
imagine its snowlit silent rooms,
pale walls icy to the touch.
Here unaccustomed thin snow
drips off the next flat's balcony.
There the grip of ice is total. And I should be there
enduring with it. Its eyes see nothing
without mine behind them. In those cold hills
a house keeps you alive. Without walls, fire,
the snow says *I am softness, immaculate,*
sink in, sleep at last.

Words in a notebook, food in the freezer,
drawers full of folded clothes, objects
and ornaments that hold my memories
wait in the reliquary of my house
that I'm cut off from. As if the one
who knew them precious had gone permanently.

House-clearance – a sad duty. Do it quickly
without thinking, taking next to nothing,
calling in the professionals. Let it not exist,
any of it. Let it not have existed.

They achieved the four-bedroomed detached house
with a nice garden. It was all she ever wanted.
Her green fingers filled the glass porch
with growing things. Then a move
nearer to family, a downsizing.
And she managed it. Found friends and interests.

When he died and the daughter moved
she needed more help: the apartment,
the cleaners and carers on hand
and again new friends among the widows.
But her front door started to shift
and when she was outside it
the way back hid itself
and people leaned out of the television.
For a while the care-home was a relief:
the meals laid on, the spacious room,
the last new ally against chaos
but chaos took her at last.
They tried a tiny room to swaddle her
and then a hospital bed and she so shrunk
she only needed a bit of it
curled there in a kind of sleep.

For the dead, home is a graveyard, a garden,
a hillside with cottongrass and thistles. For Jill
and her brother, a park bench overlooking the Sound.
Her dates 1958-2002; his, 1957 February to April.
This is no place for a baby, this enormous sea
blinding them with light, this wind
smelling of salt and frost.

Along the coast, that island off an island.
When water rolled back, the floor of the pool
shone like the pavement of heaven in jasper, cornelian,
chrysoprase, sardonyx, silver and gold,
and all those tesserae perfect miniature houses
abandoned by little lives (tellin, topshell, periwinkle)
and if one moved it was a borrowed carapace
for the nervous hermit-crab – look, the thin stems of its legs!
Living a life is difficult. A place
holds you while you try to do it.

Come back to the mainland,
in from the bright salt air
away from the insomniac sea.
This tall building echoes
with other people's lives; noise, cigarette smoke.
Dead letters on the stairs.
You wouldn't think the dead could multiply
but these do, day by day. All addressed
to here (Parr, Anastasiou, Wellfair)
but the unseen footsteps thundering up and down
ignore them. Who are Hadjuk and Schnall,
Lewis, Hitt and Holland? This house has limits,
all these many names couldn't live here,
only briefly alight like the gulls on lamps and walls
to look round and be off.

I think of my lost house hunkered down in its Arctic,
its brownish stone darkened in contrast,
its lightless eyes, the spring-water
thickening in its pipes and tanks.

I know how to live there now,
now that I'm leaving. Like people
who visit the same place every year,
who marry the same kind of man
again and again, the very same, even,
I'd like to start again (I would....I should have....)
to master it, not to be taken by surprise;
make the same poem over and over
trying to get it right.

3. Trainline

Sliding, never arriving, through England
northeast – southwest – northeast up and down
ageless countryside, snagged by brief cities.
Here, today, sunlit sheep in meadows ringed
with fresh green, a fantasy of nostalgia.

I've seen these fields softened by mist
or in the early dark of winter
absenting themselves beyond the glass
and once, everything white from Darlington to Devon.
Time hardly passes in soporific rumble and rocking.

Too cold, too hot, locked in our linked
metal boxes we're hostage to signal-failure,
engine-failure, the tree on the line,
the bomb under the bridge, unexplained
slowings and stoppings.

Always, it seems, travelling backwards
unable to see what might be approaching,
brooding over what's past and left behind
as it gets smaller and two-dimensional
and turns into someone else's story.

4. Removal

A thinning
a lightening
an emptying out.
How lovely the floor is without its clothing.

Older than trees
older than houses
older than the hills
these flagstones, bare at last in rare hot sunlight.

Dusk- or mist-grey
brownish or sandy
giant tesserae.
It's said our walls breathe in and keep some tincture of us –

what of these slabs
inscribed by currents
scribbled with wormcasts,
inlaid, this one, with sections of pale stems?

Will our ghosts tread on these seabeds gently?

5. Waste Not

(an exhibit by Song Dong at the Barbican's Curve Gallery, 2012).

The power of silent objects, things, material like us.
They kept pieces of string and crumpled brown paper.
Shelves of tinned food maturing in the pantry.
Frayed shirts cut down for children, worn sheets
turned sides-to-middle, wooden mushroom for darning.
One day I'll see if grandfather's clock could go again.

Not art, not a museum (and minus all those things
it hurt to let go of) my collection: furniture
in all shades of brown, rugs, pictures on every wall,
too many lamps, still too much china, far
more books than I shall read or read again,
taken from other rooms I remember, these possessions

make foreign spaces home. We kept what we could accommodate
of mother's clutter (aunt's, grandparents', dead friends')
to keep them slightly with us. How much will the children
in their turn, be able to fit into their lives
in their adopted countries? Perhaps they'll lay it out entire,
a work of piety, for the eyes of strangers.

The Uncertainty Principle is Inherent in the Properties of All Wave-like Systems

Even so, it's important to set out
for the island.

Concentrate on the packing: chest-waders
of course, waterproofs and woollens.

How much water you take
depends on the degree of drought.

Looking out of the window at home will tell you nothing
and weather forecasts aren't to be trusted.

When you get to the quay, the river
will only tell you the state of the tide.

Go up to Hannafore and the noise
and restlessness of the sea will disturb you.

Look over to the island: it's there, still,
untouched by the decades,

its edges slightly blurred
so that suddenly you feel unsure.

Remember the year when we waited for days
and never got across,

the sea in that strait
ridged like corrugated metal?

Go back down. You won't be surprised
when the thickset boatman stands there shaking his head.

You've seen the surf licking at Landing Beach,
whitening the Rannies, racing down from Talland.

Scratching the Surface

Needing to know what's behind, beneath.
There are legends, rumours, a rough sketch
with X marking the spot. Two carved, curved
stones in long grass. On the Armada map
a chapel balanced on the apex,

vanished now. The Time Team are digging.
They have three days (half days because of tides,
Tim's bulky boat and the limitations
of Landing Beach). Straightaway the spade
strikes stone close under the turf.

A wall. And is this a corner or an arch support?
In situ flooring, sometimes on bedrock. Here in soft ground
massive foundations. How did monks overwinter
in this wild place? Seen from the mainland
it's a small hump in a wide wide sea.

Now in the chapel-space they've found a grave. *One long
shin-bone.* Whose? *Medieval potsherds.* Broken bits,
little to show for a life, for all those centuries.
Slung round the hill, invisible except to circling gulls,
is a much older ditch. *Seven Roman coins,*

two kist burials. The island will say no more
of its long past. What's buried shouldn't be
stripped naked to daylight. Tides rise and fall like breathing,
the time is up, the programme over. Anonymous
hands will heal the hill's gashes.

Pig-sitting on the Island

The pig-pen's a quagmire after the rain.
I'm wary of stepping in. Three pigs,
a couple of hundredweight of shove and jostle,
friendly but rough. Their loose mouths and twitching snouts
muddy my legs with kisses.

The biggest one has learnt to capture the nozzle
of the hose when I aim for their water-bowl –
pleased with the clean exciting stream.
Their bodies are rounded, hot to the touch,
skins taut and black

like Brobdingnagian grapes, but clothed
in small stiff hairs. They're almost full-grown,
their death-day already decided on.
How will she feel who held the smallest one,
runt of the litter,

wrapped up and shivering on her lap?
Not long for this world – and this one's all there is.
Like summer butterflies they'll never know cold,
only the long days of island sun and showers
and the everlasting heartbeat of the sea.

Island Wedding

Blue

A ghost, it was said, a man with long fingers
stepped from the bedroom wall in a bluish haze.
And there are many ghosts moving freely here
on this blue day among the wedding guests.

She has seen the sycamore wood with a floor
of pale-blue squills, colour of spring sky.
And the midnight sea flashed sapphire phosphorescence
around them as they swam one long-ago summer.

Today, though, the sea is a tropical turquoise
and the photographs will seem almost too bright
to believe. We are gathered for the ceremony
on top of the island in the vanished chapel,

its walls transparent now, transparent
with a slight blueness like the shallows
where nets of silver flicker
and shrimps glide like solider water.

Green

Sometimes green can shine like gold. More often,
when we approach in an open boat,
it is a type of dark, the sycamore wood
hanging heavily over Landing Beach.

From the sky, the seagull's perspective,
the island is whale-shaped: blunt, humped,
with a long tail, a green thing swimming
in a sea patterned with winds and currents.

You set off from the east quay or the west.
It takes time to cross the bar, especially
in an adverse wind. On your right, high rocks.
It's ages before you get your first sighting

then you never take your eyes off it
and the boatman standing in the stern
steers his arc with a half-smile.
You will the pale beach not to disappear

as it could – figment of dream or memory.
The boatman has the power to withhold. He is
interpreter of water and wind. But if you can once
put your foot on it, the island will turn into truth.

Yellow

The dry-grass slope to the cove was shiny
and slippery as straw. When she looked back
the island could have been on fire.

She remembers lying on the yellow sand
under the sun's smile in a tickle of sandhoppers
watching a plover at the water's edge

run-along-and-stop. Run-along-and-stop.
The blinding sky above her haunted
with voices calling and singing across and across.

From Christmas the daffodil fields would be a ripple
of creamy white, yellow and spots of orange.
The sisters never managed to pick them all in time

though they loaded the boat by moonlight
and pushed it off into the gilded road.
The last of them was buried in the flower fields.

Today there is a sense of invisible busyness,
waves of warm air, benign ghosts dissolved
in sunshine: monks, smugglers, farmers, coastguards,

children, our past selves; the tall house only pretending
to be empty, its pale gold light
softened by salt and cobwebs on the glass.

The Skull

The side-view's like the island's profile
as the boat approaches: that long beak
stretching south towards the Rannies and behind it
the abrupt hill with its sycamore wood.

All the soft parts gone – what we might call the smile,
the skin supple and shining, its insulating underlay
and the brain, surely as big as ours
in that bulging skull. What's left is faceless,

yellowish, still faintly fish-smelling
after all the washing and scrubbing and rinsings of rain.
A female dolphin once, not so distant from us
with her womb and warm blood, though the mind's mysterious,

the echolocation, the language of chirps and whistles.
And it's not just the jut of bone makes the head alien –
the front looks blind, unlike a human skull
that watches you from wells of darkness.

Those who saw her whole said she was marked by the net
that stopped her looping flight through air and water.
Cast up on Landing Beach, broken and picked clean –
her only relic and memorial this bone.

Home III

1. Stranger

Planet Zog, for instance, or one with just a number
(QL154?) this place where I've landed.

The inhabitants look human: slow old men,
women with shopping bags, hooded teenagers.

A plethora of shops – odd – there's W H Smith, Boots,
Marks and Spencer. Homely but not home. And so many

people, all strangers. It's not as if I walk through
the wall of flesh, more that it parts in front of me,

closes behind, like water. Do they actually
see me? I could be a visitor from the past,

the time of reconstruction after the bombing,
or from an unimagined future. Or myself an alien

from another world: Planet Zog perhaps,
somewhere invisible to the naked eye.

2. Laughing Man

Those Polish students through my bedroom wall –
last and first thing I hear. Not music, thank God
(rap-gabble, thump of bass) only voices, lively, too loud
and from one of them, constant laughter.

Lying tense and wakeful I ill-wish him,
that happy man who responds to every day
and every coming night so unrestrainedly,
with so much bubbling joy, in his rented kitchen

among his friends. The man in Ashlake Road, though,
who laughed at any odd hour always laughed alone –
audible by day through the open window
of his room overlooking the garden. If I woke

in the small hours I'd see him in the street,
a shadow in the orange gloom, laughing
his sad, terrible laugh that echoed off
the crowded buildings of the city.

3. Towards Silence

The old house was filled with a thick quiet,
the hush of finished lives. Outside, no-one,
nothing but scarcely-moving sheep,
the passing by of wind and wings.

Here, now, I'm building barriers of glass and plaster
against the street, against the voices in the wall.
The sea has settled itself, the grey ships
approach somnambulistically.

Soon there will be no sound except the steady
hiss inside my head, my auditory shadow.

4. 'A feasting presence full of light'

I'd thought I wouldn't know the seasons any more –
bird voices always gulls' wailing. Couldn't say
I heard the first curlew or *The lapwings are back,*
couldn't tell the month by the colours of grass.
But here light is the witness.

Sun rises there or there, then or not till then,
printing the picture of the window on a wall.
Light's a presence in the room, filling the loneliness.
It's like something you can only imagine – an angel
for example, something alarming.

In the old house light was grainy, golden,
backed with shadow. Furniture dozed in the low rooms.
This sea-swollen light's not soporific, it's ice, bright knives,
kills colour, cuts into my eyes so that I turn my back,
draw blinds before I'm blinded.

5. Rooted

From the pavement, look up
through my bright room and the connecting door
to the thin window
that frames the leaning tree

inclined from right to left
like Vincent's tree over the sower,
though here the tarmac
accepts no seed.

The tree is what I mostly look at.
Behind me the sea
mosaic of mirrors
brokenly gives back whatever the sky sends

but I long for green – not that the tree has much
to offer. Like Vincent's tree it's grooved,
gnarled, with lopped stumps
and long bony fingers,

though bravely in the narrow window
it flaunts its few small swags of leaves.
When they litter the ground at the year's end
I wonder – are these the last?

Always at my back, the sea. The warships
and the big white ships go out and out smoothly
and almost silently to the invisible distances
over the horizon.

The emptiness out there dazzles my room. I fix
my mind on the crooked tree – though old
it's holding on. It leans, like the painted tree,
into its own gold sky.

6. Bay-window Triptych

Look left back to the land, through an old pane
like lumpy air, to the memorial in verdigris,
the red and white lighthouse rescued from its rock,
walkways, buildings, the edge of the marina.

It's plain glass straight ahead, so huge
you have to stand well back to view the composition.
Between near railings and far wooded cliff: blue –
it's a stage with dancers or a blue garden

with tilting coloured shoots. One of them turns
into a child's picture – two high triangles, y is for yacht.
Turns again, it's a streak of light, a white sapling. How safe
these fragile beings seem on the summer water.

My chair is set facing the right-hand view
and its dreamlike ingredients: the small island
dark with trees or mistily disappearing, complicated silhouettes
of warships – why do they wait grey and silent

out there by the breakwater and its little fort?
But what most holds the attention is the water, blue or grey
or running with white fire, passage to the open sea
that extends as far as the sky and over the edge and on perhaps for
ever.

Warships in the Sound

Not exactly grey not exactly green,
paler than the floor they float on –
the blue arena still as a stage.

Oh! that one is caught by the sun
as it shrinks across the horizon
and on to infinity.

Now one approaches, its arc
copying the bay's curve; bears down on us
in the clarity of a predator, silent

as they mostly are, though at times
a mournful bellowing surprises us.
A salute, once, in loud roundels of smoke.

When colour drains from the day
they thin and slightly darken
like rain clouds coming in.

Departure

The sound is like a kind of tinnitus –
the kind where you hear a hum and simultaneously
the little beating of your heart.

Before that: the one trumpeting roar.
Listen and watch and something will appear
between the island and the end of the road.

Millbay extrudes it slowly. It's high and white
and slides along the sea, then it swings south
quietened by the misty water,

shrinking and losing density until
it's made of breath and imagination only,
in a blurred otherworld beyond the railings.

Sub in Dock

Could be a scrap-metal shark, erect
rust-coloured fin, sloping black back.
Secretive as an iceberg, nine-tenths invisible,

tied up now but never tame.
Its raison d'être is threat, to go down
into the dark, alert for the scent of blood.

I went in one once, saw the beds big as coffins
lined up along the gut of the great fish
waiting for the swallowed sailors.

Their prophecy: the destruction of cities,
their prayer: to be belched back safe
on to the shores of daylight.

The Meet

What are they doing, clustered inside the breakwater?
A scene in greys: the horizontals of cloud,
the almost luminous sea, the distant shapes. What are they like?
Insects perhaps in their spiky oddity, or crustaceans –
antennae, claws and armour.

A rim of white behind them now, and I remember
what the boatman said. *An exercise* sounds innocent,
childish, *manoeuvres* more sinister. We saw the small
submarine tied up – its shabby back above water.
Imagine it sinking into increasing dark,

slipping out through the deepwater channel west of the lighthouse,
playing at being prey as they, the grey ships,
will play at being predators.

Yachts in Fog

If the shades in the underworld have races
to while away eternity, that's perhaps
what I'm dimly seeing:

grey on grey or greenish white,
the figures inhuman, not quite birdlike
with tall wings held vertical

milling about and disappearing, not on any floor
or water, everything's air, thick, not conducive
to breathing – they don't breathe

they're blown, silently, though there are broken echoes
of a voice and somewhere a repeated cry.
You think you glimpse wall, island

but no, there's nothing eyes can believe in,
teased by this uncertain dance of entanglements
and vanishings.

Still

Puzzled by her palette of neutrals
when she is so bright. You'd think
her element was fire, and though the pots
she paints have come through fire they wear
the phlegmatic colours of earth and water:

ivory-white amphora, grey
Japanese tea-pot, that cream
jug, the brown bottle
with brown leaves eternally paused
in their progress towards death.

I wait on the beach for the Cawsand ferry.
Sand not golden but a shade
between yellow and dust;
a distant smudge of land, mist-coloured,
hardly there; the sea fish-belly white.

The room I have left is a hall of mirrors: there
are the objects in the flesh, and there again
pictured around the walls,
pale on their pale backcloths,
cunning gradations and juxtapositions.

That plain pudding-basin
like my mother's, inherited
and used, shines it seems
with a personal light,
the apotheosis of earthenware.

I envisage her pictures
in the chaos of her room –
their absorbed stillness
as if they have lives of their own
that take up all their attention.

Louise Paints Richard's Portrait in Black and White Emulsion

Just as it's said the sculpture exists
already in the stone, so his silhouette
waits for her in the board's flat black. She needs
only to clear up the clutter of darkness.

He sits so still he seems not to be breathing.
When she looks at him it's the shape of the tone
that she interrogates, the battle
of light and dark in miniature.

Her thick pigs'-hair brush begins
a background of white or almost-white
and the shady outline of his ear appears
and the squareish crown of his head.

Here is the right side of his face
whitewashed as if he is wearing
his skull outside his skin,
its eye-socket emptied.

And now the left side in mid-grey
half there in the lamp's strong shadow.
She checks the distribution of pallor
in a hand-mirror, dots highlights like little caresses.

Meanwhile behind the man,
behind the pale cloth, the inconstant light
of midsummer intermittently
bleaches the stone wall in stripes.

Summer Art Class

Segments of sea and sky are what we mostly paint,
sometimes the same bits week on week,
but never the same. There have been
burning days, but for me today's perfect:
rain, mist, cloud, sea.

Some of us want to be artists,
I just want to be attentive,
because we're not here for long,
because already there's a lot
that my eyes miss.

Friday the 13th. A hold-up at the ferry
made us late. Fog between Antony
and Millbrook so thick I was glad
of the white line – wished we hadn't set out,
but it's clearer here.

A whole summer of making grey
and it's still not right – I'm tired of purple skies.
Ed said mix black and white, but we're not
allowed black: these gaudy blobs
our raw materials

for making shadow. White we are permitted,
ultramarine, the darker ochre,
a little alizarin. It seems hopeless
but it's a poor workman blames his tools.
Water never still,

shapeshifting vapour. We try to capture them,
this place, this time – time stopped in paint –
the various quiet greys. Truth seems too big a word
for what may come of it: these few small
glaucous rectangles.

Home IV

1. I Talked to the Trees

Exiled here where the land runs out
I turn my back on the dubious glitter
of the sea – find little comfort
in a town populated by strangers.

By now I know each tree in this scrap of a park
I visit every day – perhaps I should take up residence
like the homeless man in the shelter
behind the bamboo clump.

I wait, the bare trees wait, concentrated, attentive.
Leaves are slow to come – I know that dryness,
when roots reach out for purchase
and for sustenance and there is nothing.

The buds on the beech are narrow –
it's a long gestation – hard to believe
something is happening in such tight confines.
I want to be there for the first arrival,

to monitor the process of opening.
The leaves of the plane tree start small, a bronze
lace on the air. The beech
is surprising in olive, terracotta, flame.

Each tree becomes a city of birds and invisible insects.
Soon I shall meet people, the human race
will lay claim to me again, but I shall miss
the dialogue with trees, the intent listening.

2. Plymouth to Exeter in Three Colours

Cut off by glass from a world I could be living in:
houses in rows shrunk to children's playthings
(how small the lives must be inside them – like mine, like mine).
But look! look at the wonders among them.
How the people must stare from the little windows!
Blurry-edged like fountains that seem static
in all their energy – trees – clouds of green fire.
The word 'green' too inert for that newborn colour –
hardly a pigment, more a kind of light.

Air has no colour, sea has no colour.
They are not things but worlds, so why do we call them
blue?
Behind those clouds the spring sky is sucked pale
by sunlight, but directly overhead
it intensifies, yearning towards darkness
like the sea under its secretive lid.
As the day ticks away what might perhaps
have been thought of as blue will blacken into absence.

This place is the colour of dust to dust,
creature-colour: hair and hide – but liquid.
It's land thawed into flood – flow-country,
settled ground under a spell, at a loss,
glossy brown fields on the move
down slopes, round islands of sheep.
The train is an interruption,
creeps through on its thin embankment
to higher ground: furrowed earth striped with shine.

3. Between Scylla and Charybdis

The track's a thin braid edging the land
squeezed between cliff and sea – silver and white
last week, today thick with sediment.

The cliff's its own monster. East along the coast
the fallen tons of red-mud wall have turned
the sea bloody like Macbeth's imagining.

The train slackens speed, chatterers fall silent.
The rampart of land looms almost vertical.
Sometimes it looks like rock, knobbled, striated,

sometimes it's mud, fit to burst, fat with weeks of rain –
here splotched with greenery like mould and there
a raw plane where the surface has sheared off.

There's new mesh swaddling it and a stout-pillared
metal fence to cage us safely but we still creep past
in case our vibrations break the earth again.

The track shines with the sea's eruptions.
Fountains of spray shake the train and scatter
salt cold pellets to rattle on the windows.

4. Far to Go

If all my homes slide through the eye of my mind
at the end, death will be long-drawn-out.

A life of movement and belonging nowhere
pulled into this shape and that, giving, thinning

then stretched too far until there's a tear in the fabric
a black hole, more, reverse stars in a pale membrane

like gaps in the demented brain. By now
I'm little more than shreds snagged on the nails

of this and that loved and abandoned place,
frayed spider's web, tenacious silks.

5. Belonging

They got out just in time: Gertrud
from the Sudetenland, Karl from Estonia,
Parvati's family from Pakistan
(they were the lucky ones).

For them *home* was a word, a book of pictures,
held inside their heads, a lost possession
unrecapturable as virginity. Unrevisited
even when the world changed.

Barely touched by war and only glancingly
by hardship, mine's been a safe and peacetime life.
I know my country, but, like most of us,
not which bit of it I belong to:

my heart to one place, voice to another,
my body to a third; lost years, lost places slipped away.
Half-settled here or there and half-accepted, then up
and off again, afresh, afresh, to ever shorter futures.

6. On the Waterfront

You hear the shouting first; it sounds like danger.
I'm reading the benches – will there be space for me?
All the good places are taken, the wide views
where now the shifting clouds are slicing light
on to the sea.

The fit young men run past me up the sixty-eight steps,
along the Hoe and past the cenotaph where my friend
showed me her father's name on blackened bronze,
and headlong down past where I stand browsing
the seat-back memorials.

I drift slowly on while the runners gather and wait.
She was all I ever dreamed of. A free spirit
now at peace. Loved and missed beyond words.
The young men shoulder logs like telegraph poles,
set off again

steep down, chivvied and criticised. Some of the seats
have offerings of roses, browning lilies, carnations.
Jill and the baby, *with us for such a short time,*
had daffodils in spring in a glass vase with water
to keep them alive.

Now, a November poppy for Corporal Tony,
another for Lieutenant Commander Edwards RN.
And now the leading pole-carriers are down on the dock
and still descending, into icy water
until submerged

chest-deep in their boots and combat uniform
and out again sodden, panting back up.
A memory to laugh at in some place of dusty heat?
A man on a crutch is watching. As they pass by us
along the pavement

...

I say I'd hate to have to do that and he nods,
gestures to one of them, says 'That's my son'
who could be eighteen? twenty? The ages on the bench-plaques
vary like the names (Cyril and Damian,
Muriel and Mandy):

eighty-five, fifty, twenty-three, two months,
as do the inscriptions, two of them in Latin
like the words my children chose for their father,
for his bench inland, beside a river,
far away from here.